B.

Life Stories
Louis Braille

Peggy Burns

Illustrated by Jon Davis

Wayland

Life Stories

Louis Braille
Christopher Columbus
Anne Frank
Gandhi
Helen Keller
Martin Luther King
Florence Nightingale
Mother Teresa

Cover and frontispiece *A miniature portrait of Louis Braille, painted by Lucienne Filippi.* © **DACS 1993**.

Editor: Anna Girling
Consultant: Nigel Smith
Designer: Loraine Hayes

First published in 1993 by
Wayland (Publishers) Ltd
61 Western Road, Hove
East Sussex BN3 1JD, England

British Library Cataloguing in Publication Data
Burns, Peggy
Louis Braille.—(Life Stories Series)
I. Title   II. Series
362.41092

ISBN 0 7502 0481 8

Typeset by Dorchester Typesetting Group Ltd
Printed in Italy by G. Canale & C.S.p.A., Turin
Bound in Belgium by Casterman S.A.

Contents

Words printed in **bold** appear in the glossary.

A terrible accident

'Be careful, Louis. Don't touch the knife, it's sharp.'

Three-year-old Louis nodded and smiled up at his father, his brown eyes twinkling.

Turning away, **Monsieur** Braille began trimming leather from a saddle he was making. He earned his living by making saddles and harnesses for people in the village, near Paris in France, where they lived.

Louis rubbed a small piece of leather between his fingers, wishing he could use the tools like Papa did. The little boy

The house in the village of Coupvray where Louis grew up.

knew he must not play with the knife. Instead, he picked up an **awl**. He had seen Papa making holes in leather with this tool. Now he, too, would make holes!

4

He pressed the awl against his piece of leather. But the leather was tough. He bent his head close. Using two hands, Louis pressed the awl downwards with all his strength.

Without any warning the tool slid across the tough leather and plunged deep into the small boy's left eye.

Louis screamed loudly. Seeing the blood, Monsieur Braille frantically caught up his little boy in his arms. He ran out of the workshop into the street.

Louis's father's workshop. His tools are in the glass case.

Help — he must get help for Louis . . . But how?

The year was 1812, and **transport** was very slow. There were no buses or cars; people rode on horseback or in horse-drawn coaches.

And the nearest doctor lived many miles away!

The great doctor

A friend told Monsieur Braille about a great doctor in Paris. He decided to take Louis to see him.

They travelled all day, and Louis became more and more sick. His other eye was hurting now.

It was evening by the time they reached the doctor's rooms. The great man bent over Louis. When he had examined the eye he shook his head. 'I can do nothing, Monsieur. Only God can give him a new eye – I cannot.'

Coupvray today. It does not take long to reach Paris by train or car.

'But his other eye, doctor – at least he still has one good eye?'

Still the doctor looked serious. 'We shall see,' he said.

Blind!

The doctor asked a servant to bring a lamp, which he shone in front of Louis's eyes. The little boy did not blink. 'What do you see, Louis?' he asked.

'Nothing,' Louis sobbed. 'It's all dark.'

'I thought as much,' the doctor muttered. 'The injured eye has become **infected** – and the infection has spread to the other eye. Only time will tell whether Louis has any sight at all.'

It was a long, sad journey home. Louis cried and fretted the whole way. His eyes hurt very badly and he could see nothing.

The weeks went by. As the dreadful pain in Louis's eyes grew less, his father watched him for any signs of returning sight. There was nothing.

At last, he knew the truth. Louis would never again see the woods, the flowers, the birds. He would never be able to read and write.

Little Louis was blind.

Learning to live

The living room in Louis's house. The family cooked, ate and slept here.

The years passed. Louis gradually forgot what it was like to see. He became used to tapping his way around the village with his **cane**.

His body was thin and he was not strong, but he went to school with the rest of the village children. The teacher soon found that Louis, in spite of his blindness, was one of his cleverest pupils. The boy would lean forward in his seat, listening closely. He might not be able to read or write like the other children, but he remembered everything he was taught.

The village priest became one of Louis's best friends. The two would talk and talk, especially about **religion**.

**The village priest,
Jacques Palluy.**

'The things he asks me!' chuckled the priest to Monsieur Braille. 'You'd think he was ninety, instead of nine!' Throughout his life, Louis had a great faith in God.

One day, Louis heard of a school in Paris, called the National Institute for Blind Children.

The National Institute for Blind Children in Paris. Outside is a statue of Valentin Haüy.

'I'd like to go to this school, father,' Louis said. 'I want to learn more.'

'Don't you learn enough at the village school?' asked his father. 'Who ever heard of a blind boy learning? Learning means reading and writing, and how can you do that?'

But Louis kept asking, and in the end his father agreed. When Louis was ten years old he went to the school.

The Institute had been started in 1773 by a man called Valentin Haüy. Haüy had **invented** a **system** called **embossing**, to enable his pupils to read. He would press the shapes of large letters of the alphabet into soft paper, which the children could feel with the tips of their fingers.

A painting of the Institute in 1805.

Louis, with the other blind children, learned to read in this way. But it was oh, so slow. Louis longed to be able to read quickly, like **sighted** people did!

Valentin Haüy.

If only I could read!

Louis soon found that there was something he *could* do, and do well. The **organist** at a nearby church began to give him music lessons, and Louis soon discovered that he was very **talented**. He loved music, and practised every day.

Louis played the organ at this church.

17

At last the organist could teach him no more. Louis began to teach other blind children to play. And when he was only fifteen years old Louis became the church organist himself.

But he still wished he could read books and newspapers, as some of his sighted friends did. If only someone would think up a different way of reading and writing, specially for blind people!

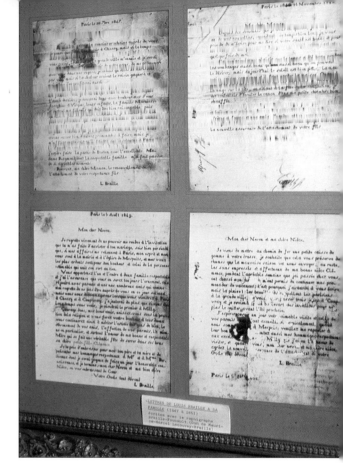

Louis learnt to write at the Institute. These are letters he wrote to his family.

Louis's own set of dominoes. He could feel the dots with his fingers.

Louis thought a lot about the problem. The embossing system of reading and writing, which he had learnt at school, was all wrong for the blind. Letters had been invented for the eye, not for the fingers!

But blind people had other **senses** – they could hear, smell, touch, taste. What if it were possible to read words by some other method that had nothing to do with the eye? A system of **mechanical** sounds, perhaps?

But how would it work? wondered Louis.

Light in the darkness

A few years earlior an officer in the French army, Captain Charles Barbier, had invented a way for his soldiers to read messages in the dark.

One day, Captain Barbier came to speak at the Institute. He talked about his reading system, which used a series of bulges punched into thick paper. The bulges could easily be felt with the fingertips.

'Something like my system could well be used to help blind people to read,' Barbier said.

Louis listened eagerly. Perhaps he himself could make the system suitable for the blind.

He set to work, trying one idea, then another. But he could not get it right. He ate only when someone reminded him. He slept little. He grew thin, and began to cough a lot. He was only fifteen years old, but during the day he taught classes at the school while night after night he worked on his reading system.

These frames are like the one Louis invented.

Reading Louis's system – using the fingertips.

At last, after a long time, he hit on the right idea – a series of dots, which he put together in groups of six, each group making a letter. Using the dots, he made up a whole new alphabet, numbers, and even music.

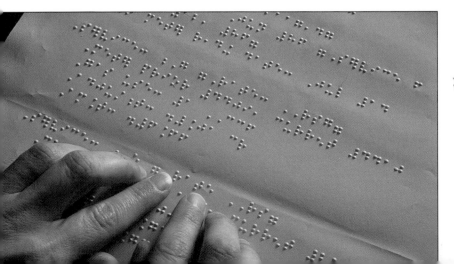

He fitted a flat piece of metal with six small holes in it into a frame. He pushed a blunt needle through the holes to make raised dots on a piece of thick paper. His fingertips swiftly read the letters the dots stood for.

Letters written in Louis's system.

A	B	C	D	E
K	L	M	N	O
U	V	X	Y	Z

The long struggle

Louis called a meeting of the school of all the teachers and pupils. Then he asked someone to read to him from a book. As the man read, Louis punched away with his needle and frame. Then he read aloud from the paper, running his fingers along the raised dots. He read back every word.

Louis had thought that the teachers would be as excited as he was. But instead they were angry.

'It's a trick!' they cried. 'Braille has **memorized**

all this. He cannot be reading from that frame!'

'But I am,' poor Louis told them. 'Test me.'

But they would not. Later, Louis found out why. The school had spent a lot of money on the embossing system. It would all be wasted if they began to teach something new.

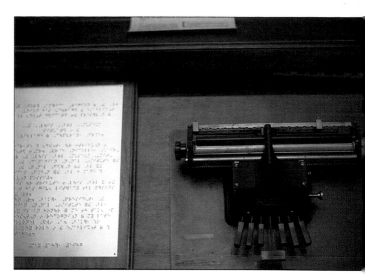

An early machine, made in the USA, for punching the dots of Louis's system.

Louis felt a failure. He was not allowed to teach his system in the school. But he did not forget about it. He paid a man to read books aloud, and he copied out in his dots everything he heard. He now had a pleasure no blind person had ever had before – he could spend hours reading and learning.

This bust gives us a good idea of what Louis looked like.

As the years went by, Louis struggled on, working to improve his system, and teaching it in secret to a few blind students. But he wanted *everybody* to know about it, and there seemed to be no way to spread the news. And the worst of it was, nobody seemed to care.

27

Success

Louis had never taken proper care of himself. He had always worked for long hours without much food or sleep, and he never seemed to be without a cough. The cough grew worse over the years, and eventually Louis became very ill with **tuberculosis**.

Louis's grave in Coupvray.

In 1852, when he was only forty-three and still struggling to make his wonderful invention known to the world, Louis died. Sadly, he never knew how successful it was to become.

In 1854, only two years after his death, Louis's invention was made the standard reading system for the blind in France. It became known simply by his name — braille.

Louis's tomb in the Panthéon.

France's heroes are buried in the Panthéon, Paris. In 1952 Louis's body was moved here.

Nowadays, braille is used in almost every country in the world.

Louis had always longed to help other blind people. He would have been thrilled to know that braille — his reading system — was to change the lives of blind people everywhere, for all time.

29

Glossary

Awl A pointed tool for making small holes.

Cane A thin stick often used by blind people to help them know when something is in their way.

Embossing An early reading method for the blind, where the shapes of letters of the alphabet were pressed into thick paper.

Infected Made unwell by the spreading of a sickness or disease.

Invented Created or thought up by a person for the first time.

Mechanical Worked by machinery.

Memorized Learnt off by heart.

Monsieur The French word for 'Mister'.

Organist A person who plays the organ — a musical instrument often played in churches.

Religion The worship of a god or gods.

Senses Sight, hearing, touch, smell and taste. Through our five senses we know what is happening in the world around us.

Sighted Able to see.

System A plan or method of doing something.

Talented Having a remarkable skill, such as being able to draw, paint, play music or write books.

Transport A way of travelling or of carrying goods.

Tuberculosis A very serious disease of the lungs.

Date chart

1809 Louis Braille is born.

1812 Louis is blinded in an accident in his father's workshop.

1819 Louis starts at the National Institute for Blind Children in Paris.

1821 Charles Barbier visits the Institute to demonstrate his night-reading system.

1824 Louis invents reading system using raised dots.

1852 6 January Louis dies of tuberculosis.

1854 Braille becomes standard reading system for the blind in France.

1952 Louis's body is taken to the Panthéon, Paris, where France's heroes are buried.

Books to read

Look at Eyes by Ruth Thomson (Franklin Watts, 1988)

Louis Braille by Beverley Birch (Exley Publications, 1990)

Louis Braille by Stephen Keeler (Wayland, 1986)

Touch by Wayne Jackman (Wayland, 1989)

Touch, Taste and Smell by Steve Parker (Franklin Watts, 1989)

Your Body: 5. Seeing, Hearing and Tasting by Dr Gwynne Vevers (The Bodley Head, 1984)

Index

Picture acknowledgements
The publishers would like to thank the
following: Explorer 15 bottom and 16
(J. Charmet); Eye Ubiquitous cover
and frontispiece, 4, 7, 8, 12, 15 top, 18
both, 22 top, 23, 25, 26, 28, 29 both;
Wayland Picture Library 14, 17; Zefa
22 bottom.